50 Premium Island Dinner Recipes for Home

By: Kelly Johnson

Table of Contents

- Coconut Curry Shrimp
- Grilled Mahi-Mahi with Pineapple Salsa
- Jerk Chicken with Mango Chutney
- Lobster Tail with Garlic Butter
- Island-Style Pork Ribs
- Caribbean Lobster Bisque
- Rum-Glazed Salmon
- Pineapple Teriyaki Chicken
- Coconut Crusted Fish
- Spicy Caribbean Beef Stew
- Grilled Pineapple and Shrimp Skewers
- Jamaican Jerk Pork Tenderloin
- Tropical Fish Tacos
- Bahamian Conch Fritters
- Cilantro Lime Chicken
- Roasted Plantains with Black Beans
- Mango and Avocado Salad with Grilled Tuna
- Island-Style Barbecue Ribs
- Caribbean Chicken and Rice
- Tamarind Glazed Duck
- Coconut Milk Fish Stew
- Pineapple and Ginger Glazed Chicken Wings
- Grilled Octopus with Citrus Vinaigrette
- Rum and Lime Marinated Pork Chops
- Caribbean Shrimp and Grits
- Tropical Stuffed Bell Peppers
- Coconut-Lime Shrimp Scampi
- Island-Style Beef and Vegetable Stir-Fry
- Calypso Chicken with Sweet Potatoes
- Grilled Swordfish with Avocado Salsa
- Spicy Coconut Curry Mussels
- Tropical Fruit and Chicken Salad

- Caribbean Spiced Lamb Chops
- Jerk Spiced Grilled Vegetables
- Pineapple Salsa with Grilled Pork
- Coconut and Mango Rice
- Seafood Paella with Island Spices
- Jamaican Beef Patties
- Tropical Grilled Chicken Skewers
- Pineapple and Coconut Stuffed Pork Tenderloin
- Grilled Fish Tacos with Tropical Slaw
- Caribbean-Style Stuffed Plantains
- Mango-Coconut Chicken Curry
- Rum-Pineapple Glazed Ham
- Spicy Island Shrimp Pasta
- Grilled Pineapple and Chicken Salad
- Coconut and Lime Poached Lobster
- Caribbean BBQ Chicken Pizza
- Pineapple and Ginger Pork Belly
- Tropical Mango Chutney Pork Tenderloin

Coconut Curry Shrimp

- 1 lb shrimp, peeled and deveined
- 1 can coconut milk
- 2 tbsp curry powder
- 1 tbsp olive oil
- 1 onion, chopped
- 3 garlic cloves, minced
- 1 red bell pepper, sliced
- 1 cup spinach
- Salt and pepper to taste
- Fresh cilantro for garnish

Instructions:

1. Heat olive oil in a pan over medium heat. Sauté onion and garlic until translucent.
2. Add curry powder and cook for another minute.
3. Pour in coconut milk and bring to a simmer.
4. Add bell pepper and cook for 3-4 minutes.
5. Add shrimp, cook until pink and cooked through.
6. Stir in spinach until wilted.
7. Season with salt and pepper.
8. Garnish with cilantro before serving.

Grilled Mahi-Mahi with Pineapple Salsa

For the Mahi-Mahi:

- 4 Mahi-Mahi fillets
- 2 tbsp olive oil
- 1 tsp paprika
- 1 tsp garlic powder
- 1 tsp onion powder
- Salt and pepper to taste

For the Pineapple Salsa:

- 1 cup fresh pineapple, diced
- 1/2 red bell pepper, diced
- 1/4 cup red onion, finely chopped
- 1 jalapeño, seeded and minced (optional for heat)
- 2 tbsp fresh cilantro, chopped
- 1 tbsp lime juice
- Salt to taste

Instructions:

1. Preheat the grill to medium-high heat.
2. **Prepare the Mahi-Mahi:**
   - In a small bowl, mix olive oil, paprika, garlic powder, onion powder, salt, and pepper.
   - Brush the mixture onto both sides of the Mahi-Mahi fillets.
3. **Grill the Mahi-Mahi:**
   - Place the fillets on the grill and cook for 3-4 minutes per side, or until the fish is opaque and flakes easily with a fork.
4. **Prepare the Pineapple Salsa:**
   - In a bowl, combine pineapple, red bell pepper, red onion, jalapeño (if using), cilantro, lime juice, and salt.
   - Mix well.
5. **Serve:**
   - Top the grilled Mahi-Mahi fillets with the pineapple salsa.
   - Serve immediately.

Lobster Tail with Garlic

- 4 lobster tails
- 4 tbsp butter, melted
- 4 garlic cloves, minced
- 1 tbsp fresh parsley, chopped
- 1 lemon, juiced
- Salt and pepper to taste

Instructions:

1. Preheat your grill or oven to 375°F (190°C).
2. **Prepare the Lobster Tails:**
    - Use kitchen scissors to cut down the top of each lobster tail, from the shell to the tail fin. Gently lift the meat out of the shell, keeping it attached at the base, and rest it on top of the shell.
3. **Prepare the Garlic Butter:**
    - Mix melted butter, minced garlic, parsley, lemon juice, salt, and pepper.
4. **Season and Cook:**
    - Brush the garlic butter mixture over the lobster meat.
    - Grill or bake for 8-10 minutes, or until the lobster meat is opaque and cooked through.
5. **Serve:**
    - Brush with additional garlic butter and garnish with more parsley if desired.

Jerk Chicken with Mango Chutney

For the Jerk Chicken:

- 4 bone-in, skin-on chicken thighs
- 2 tbsp jerk seasoning (store-bought or homemade)
- 2 tbsp olive oil
- 1 lime, juiced
- Salt to taste

For the Mango Chutney:

- 1 ripe mango, peeled and diced
- 1/2 red onion, finely chopped
- 1/4 cup sugar
- 1/4 cup white vinegar
- 1 tbsp fresh ginger, grated
- 1/4 tsp ground cinnamon
- 1/4 tsp ground cloves
- 1/4 tsp turmeric
- 1/4 tsp chili flakes (optional, for heat)
- Salt to taste

Instructions:

1. **Prepare the Chicken:**
   - In a bowl, mix jerk seasoning, olive oil, lime juice, and salt.
   - Rub the mixture all over the chicken thighs. Marinate for at least 1 hour, preferably overnight.
2. **Cook the Chicken:**
   - Preheat the grill or oven to 375°F (190°C).
   - Grill or bake the chicken thighs for 25-30 minutes, or until the internal temperature reaches 165°F (74°C) and the skin is crispy.
3. **Prepare the Mango Chutney:**
   - In a saucepan, combine diced mango, red onion, sugar, white vinegar, ginger, cinnamon, cloves, turmeric, chili flakes (if using), and salt.
   - Cook over medium heat, stirring occasionally, until the mixture thickens and becomes syrupy, about 15-20 minutes.
4. **Serve:**
   - Serve the jerk chicken hot, topped with a generous spoonful of mango chutney.

Lobster Tail with Garlic Butter

- 4 lobster tails
- 4 tbsp butter, melted
- 4 garlic cloves, minced
- 1 tbsp fresh parsley, chopped
- 1 tbsp lemon juice
- Salt and pepper to taste

Instructions:

1. Preheat your oven to 375°F (190°C) or grill to medium-high heat.
2. **Prepare the Lobster Tails:**
    - Use kitchen scissors to cut down the top of each lobster tail shell, from the base to the tail fin. Gently lift the meat out of the shell and rest it on top.
3. **Prepare the Garlic Butter:**
    - Mix melted butter, minced garlic, parsley, lemon juice, salt, and pepper.
4. **Season and Cook:**
    - Brush the garlic butter mixture over the lobster meat.
    - Bake or grill for 8-10 minutes, or until the meat is opaque and cooked through.
5. **Serve:**
    - Brush with additional garlic butter and garnish with more parsley if desired.

Island-Style Pork Ribs

For the Ribs:

- 2 racks pork ribs
- 2 tbsp olive oil
- Salt and pepper to taste

For the Island-Style Marinade:

- 1/4 cup soy sauce
- 1/4 cup brown sugar
- 2 tbsp honey
- 2 tbsp fresh lime juice
- 3 garlic cloves, minced
- 1 tbsp grated ginger
- 1 tbsp jerk seasoning
- 1 tsp allspice
- 1/2 tsp cayenne pepper (optional, for heat)

Instructions:

1. **Prepare the Marinade:**
   - In a bowl, mix soy sauce, brown sugar, honey, lime juice, garlic, ginger, jerk seasoning, allspice, and cayenne pepper.
2. **Marinate the Ribs:**
   - Rub the ribs with olive oil, salt, and pepper.
   - Place in a large resealable bag or dish and pour the marinade over the ribs. Marinate for at least 2 hours, preferably overnight.
3. **Cook the Ribs:**
   - Preheat your grill to medium heat or oven to 300°F (150°C).
   - For grilling, cook ribs over indirect heat for 1.5 to 2 hours, turning occasionally and basting with leftover marinade. For oven cooking, wrap ribs in foil and bake for 2.5 to 3 hours. Unwrap and broil for an additional 5-10 minutes for a caramelized finish.
4. **Serve:**
   - Slice and serve with additional marinade or your favorite barbecue sauce.

Caribbean Lobster Bisque

Ingredients:

- 1 lb lobster meat, chopped
- 4 cups lobster or seafood stock
- 1 cup heavy cream
- 1/4 cup tomato paste
- 1/4 cup dry white wine
- 1 onion, chopped
- 2 garlic cloves, minced
- 1 bell pepper, chopped
- 1 tbsp fresh ginger, grated
- 1 tsp allspice
- 1/2 tsp thyme
- 1/4 tsp cayenne pepper (optional, for heat)
- 2 tbsp butter
- Salt and pepper to taste
- Fresh parsley for garnish

Instructions:

1. **Prepare the Base:**
   - In a large pot, melt butter over medium heat. Sauté onion, garlic, bell pepper, and ginger until softened.
2. **Add Spices and Liquids:**
   - Stir in tomato paste, allspice, thyme, and cayenne pepper. Cook for 1-2 minutes.
   - Add white wine and cook until reduced by half.
3. **Simmer the Soup:**
   - Pour in lobster stock and bring to a simmer. Cook for 15 minutes.
4. **Blend and Finish:**
   - Using an immersion blender, blend the soup until smooth (or transfer to a blender in batches).
   - Stir in heavy cream and lobster meat. Simmer for 5-10 minutes until heated through. Adjust seasoning with salt and pepper.
5. **Serve:**
   - Garnish with fresh parsley and serve hot.

Rum-Glazed Salmon

Ingredients:

- 4 salmon fillets
- 1/4 cup dark rum
- 1/4 cup brown sugar
- 2 tbsp soy sauce
- 1 tbsp Dijon mustard
- 2 tbsp honey
- 2 garlic cloves, minced
- 1 tbsp fresh lime juice
- Salt and pepper to taste
- Fresh cilantro for garnish

Instructions:

1. **Prepare the Glaze:**
   - In a saucepan, combine rum, brown sugar, soy sauce, Dijon mustard, honey, garlic, and lime juice.
   - Simmer over medium heat until the mixture thickens and reduces by half, about 10 minutes.
2. **Season and Cook the Salmon:**
   - Preheat your grill or oven to 375°F (190°C).
   - Season the salmon fillets with salt and pepper.
   - Brush the fillets with a little bit of the glaze and cook for 12-15 minutes, or until the salmon is cooked through and flakes easily with a fork.
3. **Glaze and Serve:**
   - Brush the cooked salmon with additional glaze and garnish with fresh cilantro. Serve immediately.

Pineapple Teriyaki Chicken

Ingredients:

- 4 boneless, skinless chicken thighs
- 1 cup pineapple juice
- 1/4 cup soy sauce
- 1/4 cup brown sugar
- 2 tbsp rice vinegar
- 2 garlic cloves, minced
- 1 tbsp fresh ginger, grated
- 1 tbsp cornstarch mixed with 2 tbsp water (for thickening)
- 1 cup fresh pineapple chunks
- 2 tbsp vegetable oil
- Salt and pepper to taste
- Sliced green onions and sesame seeds for garnish

Instructions:

1. **Prepare the Teriyaki Sauce:**
    - In a saucepan, combine pineapple juice, soy sauce, brown sugar, rice vinegar, garlic, and ginger. Bring to a simmer.
    - Stir in the cornstarch mixture and cook until the sauce thickens, about 2 minutes. Remove from heat.
2. **Cook the Chicken:**
    - Season the chicken thighs with salt and pepper.
    - Heat vegetable oil in a skillet over medium heat. Cook the chicken for 6-7 minutes per side, or until cooked through and golden brown.
3. **Add Pineapple:**
    - Add pineapple chunks to the skillet and cook for an additional 2 minutes.
4. **Glaze and Serve:**
    - Brush the chicken with the teriyaki sauce and cook for another 2 minutes.
    - Garnish with sliced green onions and sesame seeds. Serve hot.

Coconut Crusted Fish

Ingredients:

- 4 fish fillets (like tilapia or cod)
- 1 cup shredded coconut
- 1/2 cup panko breadcrumbs
- 1/2 cup all-purpose flour
- 2 large eggs
- 1 tbsp milk
- Salt and pepper to taste
- 1/4 cup vegetable oil
- Lime wedges for serving

Instructions:

1. **Prepare the Coatings:**
    - In a shallow dish, mix shredded coconut and panko breadcrumbs.
    - In another dish, place flour. Season with salt and pepper.
    - In a third dish, whisk together eggs and milk.
2. **Bread the Fish:**
    - Dredge each fish fillet in flour, shaking off excess.
    - Dip in the egg mixture, then coat with the coconut-breadcrumb mixture, pressing gently to adhere.
3. **Cook the Fish:**
    - Heat vegetable oil in a skillet over medium heat.
    - Cook the fillets for 3-4 minutes per side, or until golden brown and cooked through.
4. **Serve:**
    - Serve hot with lime wedges.

Spicy Caribbean Beef Stew

Ingredients:

- 2 lbs beef stew meat, cut into cubes
- 2 tbsp vegetable oil
- 1 large onion, chopped
- 3 garlic cloves, minced
- 1 bell pepper, chopped
- 2 carrots, sliced
- 1 large potato, peeled and cubed
- 1 can (14.5 oz) diced tomatoes
- 1 cup beef broth
- 2 tbsp tomato paste
- 1 tbsp jerk seasoning
- 1 tsp allspice
- 1/2 tsp cayenne pepper (optional, for extra heat)
- 1/2 tsp thyme
- 1 bay leaf
- 1 cup frozen peas
- Salt and pepper to taste
- Fresh cilantro or parsley for garnish

Instructions:

1. **Brown the Beef:**
    - Heat vegetable oil in a large pot over medium-high heat. Add beef cubes and brown on all sides. Remove and set aside.
2. **Sauté the Vegetables:**
    - In the same pot, add onion, garlic, and bell pepper. Cook until softened.
3. **Build the Stew:**
    - Stir in carrots, potato, and tomato paste. Cook for a couple of minutes.
    - Add diced tomatoes, beef broth, jerk seasoning, allspice, cayenne pepper (if using), thyme, and bay leaf. Return the browned beef to the pot.
4. **Simmer:**
    - Bring to a boil, then reduce heat to low. Cover and simmer for 1.5 to 2 hours, or until beef is tender and the stew has thickened.
5. **Finish the Stew:**
    - Stir in frozen peas and cook for an additional 5 minutes. Adjust seasoning with salt and pepper.
6. **Serve:**
    - Garnish with fresh cilantro or parsley. Serve hot.

Grilled Pineapple and Shrimp Skewers

Ingredients:

- 1 lb large shrimp, peeled and deveined
- 1 cup fresh pineapple chunks
- 2 tbsp olive oil
- 2 tbsp honey
- 1 tbsp soy sauce
- 2 garlic cloves, minced
- 1 tsp fresh ginger, grated
- 1/2 tsp smoked paprika
- Salt and pepper to taste
- Bamboo skewers (soaked in water for 30 minutes) or metal skewers

Instructions:

1. **Prepare the Marinade:**
    - In a bowl, mix olive oil, honey, soy sauce, garlic, ginger, smoked paprika, salt, and pepper.
2. **Marinate the Shrimp:**
    - Toss the shrimp in the marinade and let sit for 15-30 minutes.
3. **Assemble the Skewers:**
    - Thread shrimp and pineapple chunks onto the skewers, alternating between the two.
4. **Grill:**
    - Preheat the grill to medium-high heat.
    - Grill the skewers for 2-3 minutes per side, or until the shrimp are pink and opaque and the pineapple has caramelized.
5. **Serve:**
    - Serve hot off the grill.

Jamaican Jerk Pork Tenderloin

Ingredients:

- 1.5 lbs pork tenderloin
- 2 tbsp olive oil
- 2 tbsp jerk seasoning (store-bought or homemade)
- 2 garlic cloves, minced
- 1 tbsp fresh thyme leaves
- 1 tbsp brown sugar
- 1 tbsp soy sauce
- 1 lime, juiced
- Salt and pepper to taste

Instructions:

1. **Prepare the Marinade:**
    - In a bowl, mix olive oil, jerk seasoning, garlic, thyme, brown sugar, soy sauce, lime juice, salt, and pepper.
2. **Marinate the Pork:**
    - Rub the marinade all over the pork tenderloin. Marinate in the refrigerator for at least 1 hour, preferably overnight.
3. **Cook the Pork:**
    - Preheat your oven to 375°F (190°C) or grill to medium-high heat.
    - For oven: Roast the pork tenderloin on a baking sheet for 25-30 minutes, or until the internal temperature reaches 145°F (63°C). For grill: Grill over indirect heat for 20-25 minutes, turning occasionally.
4. **Rest and Serve:**
    - Let the pork rest for 5 minutes before slicing. Serve with your choice of sides.

Tropical Fish Tacos

Ingredients:

For the Fish:

- 1 lb white fish fillets (such as tilapia or cod)
- 1/2 cup all-purpose flour
- 1/2 cup cornmeal
- 1 tsp paprika
- 1/2 tsp garlic powder
- 1/2 tsp onion powder
- 1/2 tsp cumin
- 1/4 tsp cayenne pepper (optional, for heat)
- Salt and pepper to taste
- 1 large egg
- 1/2 cup buttermilk or milk
- Vegetable oil for frying

For the Tropical Salsa:

- 1 cup fresh pineapple, diced
- 1/2 red bell pepper, finely chopped
- 1/4 cup red onion, finely chopped
- 1 jalapeño, seeded and minced (optional, for heat)
- 2 tbsp fresh cilantro, chopped
- 1 tbsp lime juice
- Salt to taste

For Serving:

- 8 small corn or flour tortillas
- 1/2 cup shredded cabbage or lettuce
- Lime wedges

Instructions:

1. **Prepare the Fish:**
   - In a shallow bowl, mix flour, cornmeal, paprika, garlic powder, onion powder, cumin, cayenne pepper, salt, and pepper.
   - In another bowl, whisk together egg and buttermilk.
   - Dip fish fillets into the egg mixture, then coat with the flour-cornmeal mixture.
   - Heat vegetable oil in a skillet over medium-high heat. Fry fish for 3-4 minutes per side, or until golden brown and cooked through. Drain on paper towels.

2. **Prepare the Tropical Salsa:**
    - In a bowl, combine pineapple, red bell pepper, red onion, jalapeño (if using), cilantro, lime juice, and salt. Mix well.
3. **Assemble the Tacos:**
    - Warm the tortillas in a dry skillet or microwave.
    - Place a few pieces of fried fish on each tortilla.
    - Top with shredded cabbage or lettuce and a generous spoonful of tropical salsa.
4. **Serve:**
    - Serve with lime wedges on the side for extra zing.

Bahamian Conch Fritters

Ingredients:

- 1 lb conch meat, finely chopped
- 1 cup all-purpose flour
- 1/2 cup cornmeal
- 1/2 cup finely chopped onion
- 1/4 cup finely chopped bell pepper (red or green)
- 1/4 cup finely chopped celery
- 2 garlic cloves, minced
- 2 large eggs
- 1/2 cup milk
- 1 tsp baking powder
- 1/2 tsp paprika
- 1/2 tsp ground thyme
- 1/4 tsp cayenne pepper (optional, for heat)
- Salt and pepper to taste
- Vegetable oil for frying

Instructions:

1. **Prepare the Batter:**
   - In a large bowl, mix flour, cornmeal, baking powder, paprika, thyme, cayenne pepper, salt, and pepper.
   - In another bowl, whisk together eggs and milk.
   - Combine the wet and dry ingredients, then fold in the chopped conch, onion, bell pepper, celery, and garlic until evenly mixed.
2. **Heat the Oil:**
   - Heat vegetable oil in a deep skillet or pot over medium-high heat (about 350°F or 175°C).
3. **Fry the Fritters:**
   - Drop spoonfuls of the batter into the hot oil, being careful not to overcrowd the pan.
   - Fry for 3-4 minutes, or until golden brown and cooked through. Drain on paper towels.
4. **Serve:**
   - Serve hot with a dipping sauce, like spicy mayo or a tangy hot sauce.

Cilantro Lime Chicken

Ingredients:

- 4 boneless, skinless chicken breasts
- 1/4 cup fresh lime juice (about 2 limes)
- 1/4 cup olive oil
- 3 garlic cloves, minced
- 1/4 cup fresh cilantro, chopped
- 1 tsp ground cumin
- 1/2 tsp paprika
- 1/2 tsp onion powder
- Salt and pepper to taste

Instructions:

1. **Prepare the Marinade:**
    - In a bowl, whisk together lime juice, olive oil, garlic, cilantro, cumin, paprika, onion powder, salt, and pepper.
2. **Marinate the Chicken:**
    - Place the chicken breasts in a resealable plastic bag or shallow dish.
    - Pour the marinade over the chicken and ensure all pieces are coated.
    - Marinate in the refrigerator for at least 30 minutes, preferably 2-4 hours for more flavor.
3. **Cook the Chicken:**
    - Preheat your grill to medium-high heat or your oven to 375°F (190°C).
    - For grilling: Cook the chicken for 6-7 minutes per side, or until the internal temperature reaches 165°F (74°C).
    - For oven baking: Place the chicken on a baking sheet and bake for 20-25 minutes, or until the internal temperature reaches 165°F (74°C).
4. **Serve:**
    - Let the chicken rest for a few minutes before slicing. Garnish with extra cilantro and lime wedges if desired. Serve with your choice of sides.

Roasted Plantains with Black Beans

Ingredients:

- 3 ripe plantains, peeled and sliced into 1/2-inch rounds
- 1 tbsp olive oil
- 1/2 tsp ground cumin
- 1/2 tsp paprika
- Salt and pepper to taste
- 1 can (15 oz) black beans, drained and rinsed
- 1/4 cup red onion, finely chopped
- 1/2 cup cherry tomatoes, halved
- 1/4 cup fresh cilantro, chopped
- 1 tbsp lime juice

Instructions:

1. **Roast the Plantains:**
    - Preheat your oven to 425°F (220°C).
    - Toss plantain slices with olive oil, cumin, paprika, salt, and pepper.
    - Arrange in a single layer on a baking sheet.
    - Roast for 20-25 minutes, turning halfway through, until golden and tender.
2. **Prepare the Black Beans:**
    - In a bowl, combine black beans, red onion, cherry tomatoes, cilantro, and lime juice. Mix well.
3. **Serve:**
    - Serve roasted plantains warm, topped with the black bean mixture.

Mango and Avocado Salad with Grilled Tuna

Ingredients:

For the Salad:

- 2 ripe mangoes, peeled, pitted, and diced
- 1 large avocado, peeled, pitted, and diced
- 1/2 red onion, finely chopped
- 1/2 cup cherry tomatoes, halved
- 1/4 cup fresh cilantro, chopped
- 4 cups mixed greens (such as arugula, spinach, or baby kale)

For the Grilled Tuna:

- 2 tuna steaks (about 6 oz each)
- 2 tbsp olive oil
- 1 tbsp soy sauce
- 1 tbsp fresh lime juice
- 1 garlic clove, minced
- Salt and pepper to taste

For the Dressing:

- 2 tbsp olive oil
- 1 tbsp fresh lime juice
- 1 tsp honey
- 1/2 tsp ground cumin
- Salt and pepper to taste

Instructions:

1. **Prepare the Tuna:**
    - In a small bowl, mix olive oil, soy sauce, lime juice, garlic, salt, and pepper.
    - Brush the tuna steaks with the marinade and let sit for 15 minutes.
2. **Grill the Tuna:**
    - Preheat the grill to medium-high heat.
    - Grill tuna steaks for 2-3 minutes per side for medium-rare, or longer if desired. Remove from the grill and let rest for a few minutes before slicing.
3. **Prepare the Salad:**
    - In a large bowl, combine mangoes, avocado, red onion, cherry tomatoes, cilantro, and mixed greens.
4. **Make the Dressing:**

    - In a small bowl or jar, whisk together olive oil, lime juice, honey, cumin, salt, and pepper.
5. **Assemble and Serve:**
    - Toss the salad with the dressing.
    - Top with sliced grilled tuna.
    - Serve immediately.

Island-Style Barbecue Ribs

Ingredients:

For the Ribs:

- 2 racks pork ribs
- 2 tbsp olive oil
- Salt and pepper to taste

For the Island-Style Barbecue Sauce:

- 1 cup ketchup
- 1/2 cup pineapple juice
- 1/4 cup brown sugar
- 2 tbsp soy sauce
- 2 tbsp apple cider vinegar
- 1 tbsp fresh lime juice
- 1 tbsp grated fresh ginger
- 2 garlic cloves, minced
- 1 tsp allspice
- 1/2 tsp ground cinnamon
- 1/2 tsp cayenne pepper (optional, for heat)

Instructions:

1. **Prepare the Ribs:**
    - Preheat your grill to medium heat or your oven to 300°F (150°C).
    - Remove the membrane from the back of the ribs if it hasn't been removed.
    - Rub the ribs with olive oil, salt, and pepper.
2. **Make the Barbecue Sauce:**
    - In a saucepan, combine ketchup, pineapple juice, brown sugar, soy sauce, apple cider vinegar, lime juice, ginger, garlic, allspice, cinnamon, and cayenne pepper (if using).
    - Simmer over medium heat, stirring occasionally, until thickened, about 15-20 minutes.
3. **Cook the Ribs:**
    - For grilling: Place the ribs on the grill over indirect heat. Grill for 1.5 to 2 hours, turning occasionally and basting with the barbecue sauce during the last 30 minutes.
    - For oven baking: Wrap the ribs in foil and bake for 2.5 to 3 hours. Unwrap, brush with barbecue sauce, and broil for an additional 5-10 minutes to caramelize.
4. **Serve:**
    - Let the ribs rest for a few minutes before slicing. Serve with extra barbecue sauce on the side.

Caribbean Chicken and Rice

Ingredients:

For the Chicken:

- 4 bone-in, skinless chicken thighs
- 1 tbsp olive oil
- 1 tbsp jerk seasoning (store-bought or homemade)
- 1 tsp paprika
- 1/2 tsp garlic powder
- Salt and pepper to taste

For the Rice:

- 1 cup long-grain white rice
- 1 can (14.5 oz) coconut milk
- 1 cup chicken broth
- 1/2 cup diced bell pepper (red or green)
- 1/2 cup diced onion
- 2 garlic cloves, minced
- 1 tsp fresh thyme leaves
- 1/2 tsp allspice
- 1/2 tsp turmeric (for color)
- Salt and pepper to taste

Instructions:

1. **Prepare the Chicken:**
    - Preheat your oven to 375°F (190°C).
    - Rub chicken thighs with olive oil, jerk seasoning, paprika, garlic powder, salt, and pepper.
    - Place in a baking dish and bake for 30-35 minutes, or until the internal temperature reaches 165°F (74°C) and the skin is crispy.
2. **Prepare the Rice:**
    - In a large saucepan, heat a bit of oil over medium heat. Sauté bell pepper, onion, and garlic until softened.
    - Add rice and stir for 1-2 minutes.
    - Pour in coconut milk and chicken broth. Stir in thyme, allspice, turmeric, salt, and pepper.
    - Bring to a boil, then reduce heat to low, cover, and simmer for 18-20 minutes, or until the rice is cooked and liquid is absorbed.
3. **Serve:**

    - Fluff the rice with a fork and serve alongside the baked chicken thighs. Garnish with extra thyme or cilantro if desired.

Tamarind Glazed Duck

Ingredients:

For the Duck:

- 1 whole duck (about 5-6 lbs), cleaned and patted dry
- Salt and pepper to taste
- 1 tbsp olive oil

For the Tamarind Glaze:

- 1/2 cup tamarind paste
- 1/4 cup honey
- 1/4 cup soy sauce
- 2 tbsp brown sugar
- 2 tbsp rice vinegar
- 1 tbsp fresh ginger, grated
- 2 garlic cloves, minced
- 1/2 tsp ground cumin
- 1/4 tsp ground coriander
- 1/4 tsp chili flakes (optional, for heat)

Instructions:

1. **Prepare the Duck:**
   - Preheat your oven to 375°F (190°C).
   - Rub the duck inside and out with salt and pepper.
   - Place the duck on a rack in a roasting pan, brush with olive oil, and roast for 1.5 to 2 hours, or until the skin is crispy and the internal temperature reaches 165°F (74°C).
2. **Prepare the Tamarind Glaze:**
   - In a saucepan, combine tamarind paste, honey, soy sauce, brown sugar, rice vinegar, ginger, garlic, cumin, coriander, and chili flakes (if using).
   - Simmer over medium heat, stirring occasionally, until the glaze thickens, about 10 minutes.
3. **Glaze the Duck:**
   - During the last 20-30 minutes of roasting, brush the duck with the tamarind glaze every 10 minutes, allowing the glaze to caramelize and form a sticky coating.
4. **Serve:**
   - Let the duck rest for 10 minutes before carving. Serve with additional tamarind glaze on the side.

Coconut Milk Fish Stew

Ingredients:

- 1 lb firm white fish fillets (such as cod or snapper), cut into chunks
- 1 can (14 oz) coconut milk
- 1 cup fish or vegetable broth
- 1 large onion, chopped
- 2 garlic cloves, minced
- 1 bell pepper, chopped
- 2 tomatoes, diced
- 1 cup baby spinach or kale
- 1 tbsp fresh ginger, grated
- 1 tbsp curry powder
- 1/2 tsp ground turmeric
- 1/2 tsp paprika
- 1/2 tsp cayenne pepper (optional, for heat)
- 2 tbsp olive oil
- Salt and pepper to taste
- Fresh cilantro for garnish (optional)

Instructions:

1. **Prepare the Base:**
    - Heat olive oil in a large pot over medium heat. Sauté onion, garlic, bell pepper, and ginger until softened, about 5 minutes.
2. **Add Spices and Liquids:**
    - Stir in curry powder, turmeric, paprika, and cayenne pepper (if using). Cook for 1-2 minutes until fragrant.
    - Add diced tomatoes, coconut milk, and fish broth. Bring to a simmer and cook for 10 minutes.
3. **Cook the Fish:**
    - Add fish chunks to the pot and simmer gently for 5-7 minutes, or until the fish is cooked through and flakes easily.
4. **Finish the Stew:**
    - Stir in spinach or kale and cook for another 2 minutes until wilted.
    - Season with salt and pepper to taste.
5. **Serve:**
    - Garnish with fresh cilantro if desired and serve hot with rice or crusty bread.

Pineapple and Ginger Glazed Chicken Wings

Ingredients:

For the Chicken Wings:

- 2 lbs chicken wings
- 1 tbsp olive oil
- Salt and pepper to taste

For the Pineapple and Ginger Glaze:

- 1 cup pineapple juice
- 1/4 cup soy sauce
- 1/4 cup honey
- 2 tbsp rice vinegar
- 2 tbsp fresh ginger, grated
- 2 garlic cloves, minced
- 1 tbsp cornstarch mixed with 2 tbsp water (for thickening)
- 1/4 tsp crushed red pepper flakes (optional, for heat)
- 1/4 cup chopped fresh cilantro (for garnish)

Instructions:

1. **Prepare the Chicken Wings:**
    - Preheat your oven to 400°F (200°C) or prepare a grill for medium-high heat.
    - Toss the chicken wings with olive oil, salt, and pepper.
    - Arrange the wings on a baking sheet lined with parchment paper or on the grill.
2. **Cook the Wings:**
    - Bake in the oven for 35-40 minutes, or grill for about 20-25 minutes, turning occasionally, until crispy and cooked through.
3. **Make the Pineapple and Ginger Glaze:**
    - In a saucepan, combine pineapple juice, soy sauce, honey, rice vinegar, ginger, garlic, and crushed red pepper flakes (if using).
    - Simmer over medium heat, stirring occasionally, until the mixture reduces and thickens, about 10 minutes.
    - Stir in the cornstarch mixture and cook for an additional 2 minutes until the glaze is glossy and thick.
4. **Glaze the Chicken Wings:**
    - Toss the cooked chicken wings in the pineapple and ginger glaze until evenly coated.
    - Return to the oven or grill for an additional 5 minutes if you want the glaze to caramelize further.
5. **Serve:**

- Garnish with chopped fresh cilantro and serve hot.

Grilled Octopus with Citrus Vinaigrette

Ingredients:

For the Octopus:

- 2 lbs octopus, cleaned
- 1/4 cup olive oil
- 1 lemon, juiced
- 2 garlic cloves, minced
- 1 tsp dried oregano
- 1/2 tsp smoked paprika
- Salt and pepper to taste

For the Citrus Vinaigrette:

- 1/4 cup fresh orange juice
- 2 tbsp fresh lemon juice
- 2 tbsp olive oil
- 1 tbsp red wine vinegar
- 1 tsp honey or maple syrup
- 1 tsp Dijon mustard
- 1 garlic clove, minced
- Salt and pepper to taste

Instructions:

1. **Prepare the Octopus:**
   - If using fresh octopus, bring a large pot of water to a boil. Add the octopus and cook for 30-40 minutes until tender. (If using pre-cooked octopus, skip this step.)
   - Drain and let cool slightly. Cut the octopus into manageable pieces.
2. **Marinate the Octopus:**
   - In a bowl, combine olive oil, lemon juice, garlic, oregano, smoked paprika, salt, and pepper.
   - Toss the octopus pieces in the marinade and let sit for at least 30 minutes, or up to 2 hours in the refrigerator.
3. **Prepare the Citrus Vinaigrette:**
   - In a bowl or jar, whisk together orange juice, lemon juice, olive oil, red wine vinegar, honey or maple syrup, Dijon mustard, garlic, salt, and pepper.
4. **Grill the Octopus:**
   - Preheat your grill to medium-high heat.
   - Grill octopus pieces for 2-3 minutes per side, or until they develop a nice char and are heated through.
5. **Serve:**

- Drizzle the grilled octopus with the citrus vinaigrette.
- Serve warm, garnished with extra lemon or orange slices if desired.

Rum and Lime Marinated Pork Chops

Ingredients:

For the Marinade:

- 1/4 cup dark rum
- 1/4 cup fresh lime juice (about 2 limes)
- 2 tbsp olive oil
- 2 tbsp honey
- 2 garlic cloves, minced
- 1 tbsp fresh ginger, grated
- 1 tsp ground cumin
- 1/2 tsp paprika
- 1/2 tsp dried thyme
- Salt and pepper to taste

For the Pork Chops:

- 4 bone-in or boneless pork chops (about 1-inch thick)

Instructions:

1. **Prepare the Marinade:**
    - In a bowl, whisk together dark rum, lime juice, olive oil, honey, garlic, ginger, cumin, paprika, thyme, salt, and pepper.
2. **Marinate the Pork Chops:**
    - Place the pork chops in a resealable plastic bag or shallow dish.
    - Pour the marinade over the pork chops and ensure they are well-coated.
    - Marinate in the refrigerator for at least 1 hour, or up to 4 hours for more flavor.
3. **Cook the Pork Chops:**
    - Preheat your grill or oven to medium-high heat (or about 375°F/190°C for baking).
    - For grilling: Grill pork chops for 5-7 minutes per side, or until the internal temperature reaches 145°F (63°C).
    - For baking: Place pork chops on a baking sheet and bake for 20-25 minutes, or until the internal temperature reaches 145°F (63°C).
4. **Rest and Serve:**
    - Let the pork chops rest for 5 minutes before serving to allow the juices to redistribute.
    - Serve with your choice of sides, such as roasted vegetables or a fresh salad.

Caribbean Shrimp and Grits

Ingredients:

For the Shrimp:

- 1 lb large shrimp, peeled and deveined
- 2 tbsp olive oil
- 1 tbsp Caribbean jerk seasoning (store-bought or homemade)
- 1 tbsp fresh lime juice
- 2 garlic cloves, minced
- 1/2 cup red bell pepper, chopped
- 1/4 cup green onions, chopped
- 1/2 cup coconut milk
- Salt and pepper to taste

For the Grits:

- 1 cup stone-ground grits
- 4 cups water or chicken broth
- 1/2 cup shredded sharp cheddar cheese
- 2 tbsp butter
- Salt to taste

Instructions:

1. **Prepare the Grits:**
   - In a large saucepan, bring water or chicken broth to a boil.
   - Gradually whisk in the grits, reduce heat to low, and simmer, stirring occasionally, for about 20-25 minutes, or until the grits are tender and creamy.
   - Stir in cheddar cheese and butter. Season with salt to taste. Keep warm.
2. **Prepare the Shrimp:**
   - In a bowl, toss shrimp with olive oil, jerk seasoning, lime juice, and minced garlic. Let marinate for 15-30 minutes.
3. **Cook the Shrimp:**
   - Heat a skillet over medium-high heat.
   - Add the marinated shrimp and cook for 2-3 minutes per side, or until pink and opaque.
   - Add red bell pepper and green onions to the skillet and cook for an additional 2 minutes, until vegetables are slightly softened.
   - Stir in coconut milk and cook for another 2-3 minutes, allowing the sauce to thicken slightly. Season with salt and pepper to taste.
4. **Serve:**
   - Spoon the grits onto plates and top with the Caribbean shrimp and sauce.

- Garnish with additional green onions or fresh cilantro if desired.

Tropical Stuffed Bell Peppers

Ingredients:

- 4 large bell peppers (any color)
- 1 cup cooked quinoa or rice
- 1 cup diced pineapple (fresh or canned, drained)
- 1/2 cup black beans, rinsed and drained
- 1/2 cup corn kernels (fresh, frozen, or canned)
- 1/2 cup diced red onion
- 1/2 cup diced red bell pepper
- 1/4 cup fresh cilantro, chopped
- 1/2 cup shredded cheese (cheddar or Monterey Jack)
- 1 tbsp olive oil
- 1 tsp ground cumin
- 1/2 tsp paprika
- 1/4 tsp chili powder
- Salt and pepper to taste

Instructions:

1. **Prepare the Peppers:**
    - Preheat your oven to 375°F (190°C).
    - Cut the tops off the bell peppers and remove the seeds and membranes.
    - Lightly brush the peppers with olive oil and place them in a baking dish.
2. **Prepare the Filling:**
    - In a large bowl, combine cooked quinoa or rice, pineapple, black beans, corn, red onion, diced red bell pepper, cilantro, and shredded cheese.
    - Stir in ground cumin, paprika, chili powder, salt, and pepper. Mix well.
3. **Stuff the Peppers:**
    - Spoon the filling into each bell pepper, packing it tightly.
    - Cover the baking dish with aluminum foil.
4. **Bake:**
    - Bake in the preheated oven for 30-35 minutes, or until the peppers are tender and the filling is heated through.
    - Remove the foil during the last 5 minutes to allow the tops to brown slightly.
5. **Serve:**
    - Garnish with extra cilantro if desired and serve hot.

Coconut-Lime Shrimp Scampi

Ingredients:

- 1 lb large shrimp, peeled and deveined
- 2 tbsp olive oil
- 4 garlic cloves, minced
- 1/2 cup coconut milk
- 1/4 cup fresh lime juice (about 2 limes)
- 1/4 cup chicken or vegetable broth
- 1/4 tsp red pepper flakes (optional, for heat)
- 1 tbsp fresh cilantro, chopped
- Salt and pepper to taste
- 8 oz linguine or pasta of choice (cooked according to package instructions)

Instructions:

1. **Cook the Shrimp:**
   - Heat olive oil in a large skillet over medium heat.
   - Add garlic and cook for 1 minute until fragrant.
   - Add shrimp and cook for 2-3 minutes per side, or until pink and opaque. Remove shrimp from the skillet and set aside.
2. **Make the Sauce:**
   - In the same skillet, add coconut milk, lime juice, chicken or vegetable broth, and red pepper flakes (if using). Bring to a simmer and cook for 3-4 minutes, until slightly reduced.
   - Season with salt and pepper to taste.
3. **Combine and Serve:**
   - Return the shrimp to the skillet and toss to coat with the sauce.
   - Stir in fresh cilantro.
   - Serve over cooked linguine or pasta, and garnish with additional cilantro and lime wedges if desired.

Island-Style Beef and Vegetable Stir-Fry

Ingredients:

- 1 lb beef sirloin or flank steak, thinly sliced
- 2 tbsp vegetable oil
- 1 red bell pepper, sliced
- 1 green bell pepper, sliced
- 1 cup snap peas or snow peas
- 1 cup broccoli florets
- 1/2 cup carrot slices
- 3 garlic cloves, minced
- 1 tbsp fresh ginger, grated

For the Sauce:

- 1/4 cup soy sauce
- 2 tbsp pineapple juice
- 1 tbsp brown sugar
- 1 tbsp rice vinegar
- 1 tsp sesame oil
- 1 tsp cornstarch mixed with 2 tbsp water (for thickening)

Instructions:

1. **Prepare the Beef:**
    - In a large skillet or wok, heat vegetable oil over high heat.
    - Add the sliced beef and cook until browned, about 3-4 minutes. Remove beef from the skillet and set aside.
2. **Stir-Fry the Vegetables:**
    - In the same skillet, add a little more oil if needed. Stir-fry garlic and ginger for 30 seconds until fragrant.
    - Add bell peppers, snap peas, broccoli, and carrots. Cook for 3-4 minutes, or until vegetables are crisp-tender.
3. **Make the Sauce:**
    - In a bowl, whisk together soy sauce, pineapple juice, brown sugar, rice vinegar, sesame oil, and cornstarch mixture.
4. **Combine and Serve:**
    - Return the beef to the skillet with the vegetables.
    - Pour the sauce over the beef and vegetables and stir until everything is evenly coated and the sauce thickens, about 2 minutes.
    - Serve hot over rice or noodles.

Calypso Chicken with Sweet Potatoes

Ingredients:

- 4 bone-in, skinless chicken thighs
- 2 large sweet potatoes, peeled and cubed
- 2 tbsp olive oil
- 1 tbsp Calypso seasoning (or a mix of paprika, allspice, garlic powder, and cayenne pepper)
- 1 tbsp fresh thyme leaves
- 1/2 cup chicken broth
- 1/4 cup fresh lime juice (about 2 limes)
- Salt and pepper to taste

Instructions:

1. **Prepare the Chicken and Sweet Potatoes:**
    - Preheat your oven to 400°F (200°C).
    - In a large bowl, toss sweet potato cubes with 1 tbsp olive oil, salt, and pepper. Spread them on a baking sheet.
    - Rub chicken thighs with remaining olive oil, Calypso seasoning, fresh thyme, salt, and pepper.
2. **Bake:**
    - Place chicken thighs on top of the sweet potatoes on the baking sheet.
    - Roast in the preheated oven for 35-40 minutes, or until the chicken reaches an internal temperature of 165°F (74°C) and the sweet potatoes are tender.
3. **Make the Sauce:**
    - In a small saucepan, combine chicken broth and lime juice. Bring to a simmer and cook for 5 minutes.
4. **Serve:**
    - Drizzle the lime sauce over the chicken and sweet potatoes.
    - Garnish with additional fresh thyme or lime wedges if desired.

Grilled Swordfish with Avocado Salsa

Ingredients:

For the Swordfish:

- 4 swordfish steaks (about 6 oz each)
- 2 tbsp olive oil
- 1 tbsp lemon juice
- 1 tsp dried oregano
- 1/2 tsp garlic powder
- Salt and pepper to taste

For the Avocado Salsa:

- 1 ripe avocado, diced
- 1/2 cup cherry tomatoes, halved
- 1/4 cup red onion, finely chopped
- 2 tbsp fresh cilantro, chopped
- 1 tbsp lime juice
- Salt and pepper to taste

Instructions:

1. **Marinate the Swordfish:**
   - In a bowl, mix olive oil, lemon juice, oregano, garlic powder, salt, and pepper.
   - Brush the swordfish steaks with the marinade and let sit for 15-30 minutes.
2. **Prepare the Avocado Salsa:**
   - In a medium bowl, combine diced avocado, cherry tomatoes, red onion, cilantro, lime juice, salt, and pepper. Gently toss to mix.
3. **Grill the Swordfish:**
   - Preheat your grill to medium-high heat.
   - Grill swordfish steaks for 4-5 minutes per side, or until the fish is opaque and flakes easily with a fork.
4. **Serve:**
   - Top the grilled swordfish with avocado salsa.
   - Serve immediately with your choice of sides, such as rice or a fresh salad.

Spicy Coconut Curry Mussels

Ingredients:

- 2 lbs mussels, cleaned and debearded
- 1 tbsp vegetable oil
- 1 large onion, finely chopped
- 3 garlic cloves, minced
- 1 tbsp fresh ginger, grated
- 2 tbsp red curry paste
- 1 can (14 oz) coconut milk
- 1/2 cup chicken or vegetable broth
- 1 tbsp fish sauce
- 1 tbsp brown sugar
- 1 lime, juiced
- 1/4 cup fresh cilantro, chopped (for garnish)
- 1-2 red chili peppers, sliced (optional, for extra heat)
- Salt and pepper to taste

Instructions:

1. **Prepare the Mussels:**
   - Rinse mussels under cold water, scrubbing the shells and removing any beards. Discard any that are open and do not close when tapped.
2. **Make the Curry Sauce:**
   - Heat vegetable oil in a large pot over medium heat.
   - Add onion and cook until softened, about 5 minutes.
   - Stir in garlic and ginger, and cook for 1 minute until fragrant.
   - Add red curry paste and cook for 2 minutes, stirring frequently.
   - Pour in coconut milk, chicken or vegetable broth, fish sauce, and brown sugar. Stir well and bring to a simmer.
3. **Cook the Mussels:**
   - Add the cleaned mussels to the pot.
   - Cover and cook for 5-7 minutes, or until the mussels have opened. Discard any mussels that remain closed.
4. **Finish and Serve:**
   - Stir in lime juice and season with salt and pepper to taste.
   - Garnish with fresh cilantro and sliced red chili peppers if desired.
   - Serve the mussels with the curry sauce, along with crusty bread or rice to soak up the flavorful broth.

Tropical Fruit and Chicken Salad

Ingredients:

- 2 cups cooked chicken breast, shredded or diced
- 1 cup pineapple chunks (fresh or canned, drained)
- 1 cup mango chunks
- 1/2 cup sliced strawberries
- 1/2 cup sliced kiwi
- 1/4 cup red onion, thinly sliced
- 1/4 cup fresh cilantro, chopped
- 4 cups mixed salad greens

For the Dressing:

- 1/4 cup olive oil
- 2 tbsp fresh lime juice
- 1 tbsp honey
- 1 tsp Dijon mustard
- Salt and pepper to taste

Instructions:

1. **Prepare the Dressing:**
    - In a small bowl or jar, whisk together olive oil, lime juice, honey, Dijon mustard, salt, and pepper until well combined.
2. **Assemble the Salad:**
    - In a large bowl, combine mixed salad greens, chicken, pineapple, mango, strawberries, kiwi, red onion, and cilantro.
3. **Toss and Serve:**
    - Drizzle the dressing over the salad and gently toss to combine.
    - Serve immediately or chill for 15-20 minutes to allow flavors to meld.

Caribbean Spiced Lamb Chops

Ingredients:

- 8 lamb chops (about 1-inch thick)
- 2 tbsp olive oil
- 2 tbsp Caribbean spice blend (or a mix of allspice, paprika, garlic powder, cumin, and thyme)
- 1 tbsp fresh lime juice
- 3 garlic cloves, minced
- Salt and pepper to taste

Instructions:

1. **Prepare the Marinade:**
   - In a bowl, mix olive oil, Caribbean spice blend, lime juice, minced garlic, salt, and pepper.
2. **Marinate the Lamb Chops:**
   - Rub the lamb chops with the marinade, ensuring they are well coated.
   - Cover and marinate in the refrigerator for at least 1 hour, or up to 4 hours for more flavor.
3. **Cook the Lamb Chops:**
   - Preheat your grill or a skillet over medium-high heat.
   - Grill or sear the lamb chops for 4-5 minutes per side, or until they reach your desired level of doneness (medium-rare is about 135°F/57°C).
4. **Rest and Serve:**
   - Let the lamb chops rest for 5 minutes before serving.
   - Serve with a side of rice, vegetables, or a fresh salad.

Jerk Spiced Grilled Vegetables

Ingredients:

- 1 red bell pepper, sliced
- 1 yellow bell pepper, sliced
- 1 zucchini, sliced
- 1 red onion, sliced
- 1 cup cherry tomatoes
- 2 tbsp olive oil
- 2 tbsp jerk seasoning (store-bought or homemade)
- 1 tbsp fresh lime juice
- Salt and pepper to taste
- Fresh cilantro for garnish (optional)

Instructions:

1. **Prepare the Vegetables:**
   - In a large bowl, combine sliced bell peppers, zucchini, red onion, and cherry tomatoes.
   - Toss with olive oil, jerk seasoning, lime juice, salt, and pepper until evenly coated.
2. **Grill the Vegetables:**
   - Preheat your grill to medium-high heat.
   - Arrange the vegetables on the grill in a single layer.
   - Grill for 3-5 minutes per side, or until tender and slightly charred.
3. **Serve:**
   - Remove from the grill and garnish with fresh cilantro if desired.
   - Serve warm as a side dish or over a bed of rice or quinoa.

Pineapple Salsa with Grilled Pork

Ingredients:

For the Pineapple Salsa:

- 1 cup fresh pineapple, diced
- 1/2 cup red bell pepper, finely chopped
- 1/4 cup red onion, finely chopped
- 1/4 cup fresh cilantro, chopped
- 1 jalapeño, seeded and minced (optional, for heat)
- 2 tbsp lime juice
- Salt and pepper to taste

For the Grilled Pork:

- 1 lb pork tenderloin or pork chops
- 2 tbsp olive oil
- 1 tbsp paprika
- 1 tsp ground cumin
- 1/2 tsp garlic powder
- 1/2 tsp onion powder
- Salt and pepper to taste

Instructions:

1. **Prepare the Pineapple Salsa:**
    - In a bowl, combine diced pineapple, red bell pepper, red onion, cilantro, and jalapeño (if using).
    - Add lime juice and season with salt and pepper to taste.
    - Stir well and let sit for at least 15 minutes to allow flavors to meld.
2. **Prepare the Pork:**
    - Preheat your grill to medium-high heat.
    - Rub pork tenderloin or chops with olive oil, paprika, cumin, garlic powder, onion powder, salt, and pepper.
3. **Grill the Pork:**
    - Grill the pork for 5-7 minutes per side, or until the internal temperature reaches 145°F (63°C) for tenderloin or 160°F (71°C) for chops.
    - Let the pork rest for 5 minutes before slicing.
4. **Serve:**
    - Slice the grilled pork and serve with a generous topping of pineapple salsa.
    - Accompany with your choice of sides, such as rice, beans, or a fresh salad.

Coconut and Mango Rice

Ingredients:

- 1 cup jasmine or basmati rice
- 1 can (14 oz) coconut milk
- 1/2 cup water
- 1/2 cup diced ripe mango
- 1 tbsp brown sugar or honey
- 1/4 tsp salt
- 1/4 cup chopped fresh cilantro (optional)

Instructions:

1. **Cook the Rice:**
    - Rinse the rice under cold water until the water runs clear.
    - In a saucepan, combine coconut milk, water, brown sugar or honey, and salt. Bring to a boil.
    - Add the rinsed rice, reduce heat to low, cover, and simmer for 15-20 minutes, or until the rice is tender and the liquid is absorbed.
2. **Add Mango:**
    - Gently fold in the diced mango once the rice is cooked and fluffed.
3. **Finish and Serve:**
    - Stir in chopped cilantro if desired.
    - Serve warm as a side dish with grilled meats or seafood.

Seafood Paella with Island Spices

Ingredients:

- 1/4 cup olive oil
- 1 onion, chopped
- 3 garlic cloves, minced
- 1 red bell pepper, chopped
- 1 cup short-grain rice (such as Arborio or paella rice)
- 1/2 tsp smoked paprika
- 1/2 tsp ground cumin
- 1/2 tsp dried thyme
- 1/4 tsp cayenne pepper (optional, for heat)
- 1/4 tsp saffron threads (optional, for color and flavor)
- 1 can (14 oz) diced tomatoes
- 2 cups chicken or seafood broth
- 1 cup frozen peas
- 1/2 lb shrimp, peeled and deveined
- 1/2 lb mussels, cleaned
- 1/2 lb clams, cleaned
- 1/2 cup fresh parsley, chopped
- 1 lemon, cut into wedges

Instructions:

1. **Prepare the Base:**
    - Heat olive oil in a large paella pan or skillet over medium heat.
    - Add onion and cook until softened, about 5 minutes.
    - Stir in garlic and red bell pepper, and cook for another 2 minutes.
2. **Cook the Rice:**
    - Add rice, smoked paprika, cumin, thyme, cayenne (if using), and saffron (if using). Stir to coat the rice with the spices.
    - Add diced tomatoes and broth. Bring to a simmer and cook for 15 minutes, stirring occasionally.
3. **Add Seafood:**
    - Stir in peas, shrimp, mussels, and clams.
    - Cover and cook for another 5-7 minutes, or until the seafood is cooked through and the shells have opened. Discard any unopened shells.
4. **Finish and Serve:**
    - Garnish with fresh parsley and serve with lemon wedges on the side.

Jamaican Beef Patties

Ingredients:

For the Filling:

- 1 lb ground beef
- 1 tbsp vegetable oil
- 1 onion, finely chopped
- 2 garlic cloves, minced
- 1 tbsp fresh ginger, grated
- 1 tbsp Jamaican jerk seasoning
- 1/2 tsp ground allspice
- 1/2 tsp paprika
- 1/4 cup beef broth
- 1/4 cup breadcrumbs
- Salt and pepper to taste

For the Dough:

- 2 1/2 cups all-purpose flour
- 1/2 tsp salt
- 1/2 tsp turmeric (for color)
- 1/2 cup cold unsalted butter, cut into small pieces
- 1 large egg
- 1/4 cup cold water (more if needed)

Instructions:

1. **Prepare the Filling:**
   - Heat oil in a skillet over medium heat.
   - Add onion and cook until softened, about 5 minutes.
   - Stir in garlic and ginger, and cook for 1 minute.
   - Add ground beef, jerk seasoning, allspice, and paprika. Cook until beef is browned and fully cooked.
   - Stir in beef broth and breadcrumbs. Cook until the mixture is thickened. Season with salt and pepper. Let cool.
2. **Prepare the Dough:**
   - In a bowl, whisk together flour, salt, and turmeric.
   - Cut in butter until the mixture resembles coarse crumbs.
   - Beat the egg and add to the mixture with cold water. Stir until a dough forms. Add more water if needed.
   - Knead the dough lightly, then wrap in plastic wrap and refrigerate for 30 minutes.
3. **Assemble the Patties:**
   - Preheat your oven to 375°F (190°C).

- Roll out the dough on a floured surface to about 1/8-inch thickness.
- Cut into circles using a cookie cutter or a glass (about 4-5 inches in diameter).
- Place a spoonful of the beef mixture in the center of each dough circle.
- Fold the dough over the filling to form a half-moon shape and crimp the edges with a fork to seal.

4. **Bake:**
    - Place the patties on a baking sheet lined with parchment paper.
    - Brush with a beaten egg for a golden finish.
    - Bake for 20-25 minutes, or until the crust is golden brown.

5. **Serve:**
    - Let cool slightly before serving. Enjoy warm.

Tropical Grilled Chicken Skewers

Ingredients:

- 1 lb chicken breast, cut into bite-sized pieces
- 1/2 cup pineapple juice
- 1/4 cup soy sauce
- 2 tbsp honey
- 2 tbsp olive oil
- 2 garlic cloves, minced
- 1 tbsp fresh ginger, grated
- 1/2 tsp ground cumin
- 1/4 tsp red pepper flakes (optional, for heat)
- 1 red bell pepper, cut into chunks
- 1 yellow bell pepper, cut into chunks
- 1 small red onion, cut into chunks
- Fresh cilantro or parsley for garnish (optional)

Instructions:

1. **Marinate the Chicken:**
   - In a bowl, whisk together pineapple juice, soy sauce, honey, olive oil, garlic, ginger, cumin, and red pepper flakes.
   - Add chicken pieces and marinate in the refrigerator for at least 1 hour, or up to 4 hours for more flavor.
2. **Prepare the Skewers:**
   - Preheat your grill to medium-high heat.
   - Thread marinated chicken, bell peppers, and red onion onto skewers, alternating between the chicken and vegetables.
3. **Grill the Skewers:**
   - Grill skewers for 10-12 minutes, turning occasionally, until the chicken is cooked through and has an internal temperature of 165°F (74°C) and the vegetables are tender.
4. **Serve:**
   - Garnish with fresh cilantro or parsley if desired.
   - Serve hot with a side of rice or a fresh salad.

Pineapple and Coconut Stuffed Pork Tenderloin

Ingredients:

For the Stuffing:

- 1 cup fresh pineapple, finely chopped
- 1/2 cup shredded coconut
- 1/4 cup finely chopped red bell pepper
- 1/4 cup finely chopped red onion
- 1 tbsp fresh cilantro, chopped
- 1 tbsp olive oil
- 1 tbsp honey
- Salt and pepper to taste

For the Pork Tenderloin:

- 1 1/2 lbs pork tenderloin
- 2 tbsp olive oil
- 1 tbsp fresh rosemary, chopped (or 1 tsp dried rosemary)
- 1 tbsp fresh thyme, chopped (or 1 tsp dried thyme)
- 2 garlic cloves, minced
- Salt and pepper to taste

Instructions:

1. **Prepare the Stuffing:**
   - In a bowl, combine pineapple, shredded coconut, red bell pepper, red onion, cilantro, olive oil, honey, salt, and pepper. Mix well and set aside.
2. **Prepare the Pork Tenderloin:**
   - Preheat your oven to 375°F (190°C).
   - Carefully cut the pork tenderloin lengthwise, creating a pocket without cutting all the way through.
   - Season the outside of the tenderloin with olive oil, rosemary, thyme, garlic, salt, and pepper.
3. **Stuff the Tenderloin:**
   - Spoon the pineapple and coconut mixture into the pocket of the tenderloin, packing it tightly.
   - Use toothpicks or kitchen twine to secure the openings and hold the stuffing in place.
4. **Sear and Roast:**
   - Heat a skillet over medium-high heat and add a little olive oil.
   - Sear the stuffed tenderloin for 3-4 minutes on each side, until browned.

- Transfer the seared tenderloin to a baking dish and roast in the preheated oven for 20-25 minutes, or until the internal temperature reaches 145°F (63°C).

5. **Rest and Serve:**
    - Let the pork rest for 5 minutes before slicing.
    - Serve sliced with your choice of sides, such as rice, roasted vegetables, or a fresh salad.

Grilled Fish Tacos with Tropical Slaw

For the Fish Tacos:

- 1 lb white fish fillets (like cod, tilapia, or mahi-mahi)
- 2 tbsp olive oil
- 1 tbsp lime juice
- 1 tsp chili powder
- 1 tsp ground cumin
- 1/2 tsp paprika
- Salt and pepper to taste
- 8 small tortillas (corn or flour)

For the Tropical Slaw:

- 2 cups shredded cabbage
- 1 cup shredded carrots
- 1/2 cup diced mango
- 1/2 cup diced pineapple
- 1/4 cup red onion, thinly sliced
- 2 tbsp fresh cilantro, chopped
- 2 tbsp lime juice
- 1 tbsp honey
- Salt and pepper to taste

Instructions:

1. **Prepare the Fish:**
   - Preheat your grill to medium-high heat.
   - In a bowl, mix olive oil, lime juice, chili powder, cumin, paprika, salt, and pepper.
   - Brush the fish fillets with the spice mixture.
2. **Grill the Fish:**
   - Grill fish for 3-4 minutes per side, or until the fish is opaque and flakes easily with a fork. Remove from the grill and flake into large pieces.
3. **Prepare the Tropical Slaw:**
   - In a large bowl, combine shredded cabbage, shredded carrots, mango, pineapple, red onion, and cilantro.
   - In a small bowl, whisk together lime juice, honey, salt, and pepper. Pour over the slaw and toss to coat.
4. **Assemble the Tacos:**
   - Warm the tortillas on the grill or in a skillet.
   - Fill each tortilla with grilled fish and top with tropical slaw.
5. **Serve:**

- Serve immediately with extra lime wedges and fresh cilantro if desired.

Caribbean-Style Stuffed Plantains

Ingredients:

For the Stuffed Plantains:

- 4 ripe plantains (yellow with some black spots, not green)
- 2 tbsp vegetable oil (for frying)

For the Filling:

- 1/2 lb ground beef or chicken
- 1 tbsp vegetable oil
- 1/2 onion, finely chopped
- 2 garlic cloves, minced
- 1/2 bell pepper, finely chopped
- 1/2 cup canned diced tomatoes
- 1/4 cup raisins
- 1/4 cup olives, sliced
- 1 tsp ground cumin
- 1 tsp paprika
- 1/2 tsp allspice
- Salt and pepper to taste

For Garnish:

- Fresh cilantro or parsley, chopped (optional)

Instructions:

1. **Prepare the Plantains:**
    - Preheat your oven to 375°F (190°C).
    - Peel the plantains and cut them in half lengthwise.
    - Heat vegetable oil in a skillet over medium heat.
    - Fry the plantain halves for 2-3 minutes on each side, until golden brown. Remove and drain on paper towels.
2. **Prepare the Filling:**
    - In a skillet, heat 1 tbsp vegetable oil over medium heat.
    - Add onion and cook until softened, about 5 minutes.
    - Stir in garlic and bell pepper, and cook for 2 more minutes.
    - Add ground beef or chicken, and cook until browned and cooked through.
    - Stir in diced tomatoes, raisins, olives, cumin, paprika, allspice, salt, and pepper. Cook for 5 minutes, allowing flavors to meld.
3. **Stuff the Plantains:**

- Use a spoon to carefully scoop out some of the flesh from the center of each plantain half, creating a small well.
- Fill each plantain half with the prepared filling.

4. **Bake:**
   - Place the stuffed plantains on a baking sheet.
   - Bake in the preheated oven for 10-15 minutes, until heated through and slightly crisp on the edges.

5. **Serve:**
   - Garnish with fresh cilantro or parsley if desired.
   - Serve warm as an appetizer or main dish with a side of rice or salad.

Mango-Coconut Chicken Curry

Ingredients:

- 1 lb chicken breast or thighs, cut into bite-sized pieces
- 1 tbsp vegetable oil
- 1 onion, finely chopped
- 3 garlic cloves, minced
- 1 tbsp fresh ginger, grated
- 2 tbsp curry powder
- 1/2 tsp ground turmeric
- 1/2 tsp ground cumin
- 1/4 tsp cayenne pepper (optional, for heat)
- 1 can (14 oz) coconut milk
- 1 cup diced mango (fresh or frozen, thawed)
- 1/2 cup chicken broth
- 1 tbsp lime juice
- Salt and pepper to taste
- Fresh cilantro for garnish

Instructions:

1. **Cook the Chicken:**
    - Heat vegetable oil in a large skillet or saucepan over medium heat.
    - Add onion and cook until softened, about 5 minutes.
    - Stir in garlic and ginger, and cook for 1 minute until fragrant.
2. **Add Spices:**
    - Add curry powder, turmeric, cumin, and cayenne pepper (if using). Cook for 1-2 minutes, stirring constantly, until the spices are fragrant.
3. **Add Chicken:**
    - Add the chicken pieces to the skillet and cook until no longer pink on the outside, about 5-7 minutes.
4. **Add Coconut Milk and Mango:**
    - Pour in the coconut milk and chicken broth, stirring to combine.
    - Add the diced mango and bring the mixture to a simmer.
5. **Simmer:**
    - Reduce heat to low and simmer for 15-20 minutes, or until the chicken is cooked through and the sauce has thickened. Stir occasionally.
6. **Finish:**
    - Stir in lime juice and season with salt and pepper to taste.
7. **Serve:**
    - Garnish with fresh cilantro.
    - Serve hot over rice or with naan bread.

Rum-Pineapple Glazed Ham

Ingredients:

- 1 fully cooked ham (about 8-10 lbs)
- 1 cup pineapple juice
- 1/2 cup dark rum
- 1/2 cup brown sugar
- 1/4 cup honey
- 2 tbsp Dijon mustard
- 1/2 tsp ground cloves
- 1/2 tsp ground cinnamon
- Pineapple slices and maraschino cherries for garnish (optional)

Instructions:

1. **Prepare the Ham:**
    - Preheat your oven to 325°F (165°C).
    - Place the ham in a roasting pan and cover loosely with foil.
2. **Make the Glaze:**
    - In a saucepan, combine pineapple juice, dark rum, brown sugar, honey, Dijon mustard, cloves, and cinnamon.
    - Bring to a boil over medium heat, then reduce to a simmer and cook until the glaze has thickened slightly, about 10 minutes.
3. **Glaze the Ham:**
    - Remove the foil from the ham and brush a generous amount of glaze over the surface.
    - Bake uncovered for about 1 1/2 to 2 hours, or until heated through, basting with additional glaze every 30 minutes.
4. **Finish and Garnish:**
    - During the last 15 minutes of baking, arrange pineapple slices and maraschino cherries on the ham, securing them with toothpicks if needed.
    - Brush with more glaze.
5. **Serve:**
    - Let the ham rest for 10-15 minutes before carving.
    - Serve with extra glaze on the side.

Spicy Island Shrimp Pasta

Ingredients:

- 8 oz pasta (penne, linguine, or your choice)
- 1 lb large shrimp, peeled and deveined
- 2 tbsp olive oil
- 1 red bell pepper, sliced
- 1 green bell pepper, sliced
- 1 small onion, sliced
- 3 garlic cloves, minced
- 1 can (14 oz) diced tomatoes
- 1/2 cup coconut milk
- 1-2 tbsp Caribbean jerk seasoning (adjust to taste)
- 1/2 tsp crushed red pepper flakes (optional, for extra heat)
- 1/2 cup fresh cilantro, chopped
- 1 tbsp fresh lime juice
- Salt and pepper to taste

Instructions:

1. **Cook the Pasta:**
   - Cook pasta according to package instructions until al dente. Drain and set aside.
2. **Prepare the Shrimp:**
   - In a large skillet, heat olive oil over medium heat.
   - Add shrimp and cook for 2-3 minutes per side, until pink and cooked through. Remove shrimp from the skillet and set aside.
3. **Make the Sauce:**
   - In the same skillet, add sliced bell peppers and onion. Cook until softened, about 5 minutes.
   - Stir in minced garlic and cook for another 1 minute.
   - Add diced tomatoes, coconut milk, jerk seasoning, and crushed red pepper flakes (if using). Stir well and let simmer for 5 minutes.
4. **Combine and Finish:**
   - Return the cooked shrimp to the skillet and stir to coat with the sauce. Cook for another 2 minutes.
   - Add the cooked pasta and toss to combine and heat through.
   - Stir in fresh lime juice and chopped cilantro. Season with salt and pepper to taste.
5. **Serve:**
   - Serve hot, garnished with additional cilantro and lime wedges if desired.

Grilled Pineapple and Chicken Salad

Ingredients:

- 2 boneless, skinless chicken breasts
- 2 cups pineapple chunks (fresh or canned)
- 2 tbsp olive oil
- 1 tbsp honey
- 1 tbsp soy sauce
- 1 tsp smoked paprika
- 4 cups mixed salad greens
- 1/2 red onion, thinly sliced
- 1/2 cup cherry tomatoes, halved
- 1/4 cup crumbled feta cheese (optional)
- Fresh cilantro or basil for garnish (optional)

For the Dressing:

- 3 tbsp olive oil
- 2 tbsp balsamic vinegar
- 1 tbsp lime juice
- 1 tsp Dijon mustard
- Salt and pepper to taste

Instructions:

1. **Prepare the Chicken:**
    - Preheat your grill to medium-high heat.
    - In a small bowl, mix olive oil, honey, soy sauce, and smoked paprika.
    - Brush the chicken breasts with the mixture and season with salt and pepper.
    - Grill chicken for 6-8 minutes per side, or until fully cooked (internal temperature should be 165°F/74°C). Let rest for 5 minutes before slicing.
2. **Grill the Pineapple:**
    - Thread pineapple chunks onto skewers or use a grill basket.
    - Grill pineapple for 2-3 minutes per side, until caramelized and slightly charred.
3. **Prepare the Salad:**
    - In a large bowl, toss mixed greens with red onion, cherry tomatoes, and feta cheese if using.
4. **Make the Dressing:**
    - Whisk together olive oil, balsamic vinegar, lime juice, Dijon mustard, salt, and pepper.
5. **Assemble and Serve:**
    - Slice the grilled chicken and arrange it on top of the salad along with grilled pineapple.
    - Drizzle with dressing and garnish with fresh cilantro or basil if desired.
    - Serve immediately.

Coconut and Lime Poached Lobster

Ingredients:

- 2 lobster tails (about 6-8 oz each)
- 1 can (14 oz) coconut milk
- 1 cup fish or chicken broth
- 2 tbsp fresh lime juice
- 2 garlic cloves, minced
- 1 tbsp fresh ginger, grated
- 1-2 Thai chilies or red chili flakes (optional, for heat)
- 1 tbsp brown sugar
- 1/4 cup fresh cilantro, chopped
- Salt and pepper to taste

Instructions:

1. **Prepare the Lobster:**
    - Preheat your oven to 375°F (190°C) if finishing in the oven.
    - Cut the lobster tails lengthwise down the middle, or leave them whole if you prefer.
2. **Make the Poaching Liquid:**
    - In a large saucepan, combine coconut milk, fish or chicken broth, lime juice, garlic, ginger, chilies (if using), and brown sugar.
    - Bring to a simmer over medium heat, stirring occasionally.
3. **Poach the Lobster:**
    - Add the lobster tails to the simmering liquid.
    - Cook for 5-7 minutes, or until the lobster meat is opaque and cooked through. Avoid overcooking.
4. **Finish and Serve:**
    - Remove the lobster from the poaching liquid and season with salt and pepper.
    - Garnish with fresh cilantro.
    - Serve hot with extra lime wedges and the poaching liquid on the side for drizzling.

Caribbean BBQ Chicken Pizza

Ingredients:

For the Pizza:

- 1 pizza dough (store-bought or homemade)
- 1 cup cooked chicken, shredded or diced
- 1/2 cup barbecue sauce (Caribbean-style if available)
- 1/2 cup red onion, thinly sliced
- 1/2 cup red bell pepper, thinly sliced
- 1 cup shredded mozzarella cheese
- 1/2 cup shredded cheddar cheese
- 1/4 cup fresh cilantro, chopped (for garnish)

Instructions:

1. **Preheat Oven:**
    - Preheat your oven to 475°F (245°C). If you have a pizza stone, place it in the oven while it preheats.
2. **Prepare the Dough:**
    - Roll out the pizza dough on a floured surface to your desired thickness.
    - Transfer the dough to a parchment-lined pizza peel or baking sheet.
3. **Assemble the Pizza:**
    - Spread barbecue sauce evenly over the dough, leaving a small border around the edges.
    - Scatter shredded chicken over the sauce.
    - Add red onion and red bell pepper slices on top of the chicken.
    - Sprinkle shredded mozzarella and cheddar cheese evenly over the toppings.
4. **Bake:**
    - Slide the pizza onto the preheated pizza stone or bake directly on the baking sheet.
    - Bake for 12-15 minutes, or until the crust is golden and the cheese is bubbly and melted.
5. **Garnish and Serve:**
    - Remove the pizza from the oven and let it cool slightly.
    - Sprinkle fresh cilantro over the top.
    - Slice and serve hot.

Enjoy your flavorful Caribbean BBQ Chicken Pizza!

Pineapple and Ginger Pork Belly

Ingredients:

- 2 lbs pork belly
- 1 cup pineapple juice
- 1/4 cup soy sauce
- 1/4 cup brown sugar
- 2 tbsp fresh ginger, grated
- 3 garlic cloves, minced
- 1 tbsp rice vinegar
- 1 tsp sesame oil
- 1/2 tsp ground black pepper
- 1/2 tsp ground cinnamon
- 1/2 tsp ground cloves
- 1/2 cup pineapple chunks (fresh or canned)
- 2 green onions, chopped (for garnish)
- Sesame seeds (for garnish, optional)

Instructions:

1. **Prepare the Pork Belly:**
    - Preheat your oven to 325°F (163°C).
    - Score the skin of the pork belly in a crosshatch pattern with a sharp knife. This helps the fat render and the skin crisp up.
    - Pat the pork belly dry with paper towels.
2. **Make the Marinade:**
    - In a bowl, combine pineapple juice, soy sauce, brown sugar, grated ginger, minced garlic, rice vinegar, sesame oil, black pepper, cinnamon, and cloves. Mix well.
3. **Marinate the Pork Belly:**
    - Place the pork belly in a large resealable plastic bag or a dish. Pour the marinade over the pork belly, ensuring it is well coated.
    - Seal the bag or cover the dish and refrigerate for at least 2 hours, or overnight for best results.
4. **Roast the Pork Belly:**
    - Remove the pork belly from the marinade, allowing excess marinade to drip off.
    - Place the pork belly on a rack in a roasting pan. Roast in the preheated oven for 2 to 2.5 hours, or until the skin is crispy and the meat is tender.
    - During the last 30 minutes of roasting, add pineapple chunks to the roasting pan to caramelize.
5. **Finish and Serve:**

- Remove the pork belly from the oven and let it rest for 10-15 minutes before slicing.
- Garnish with chopped green onions and sesame seeds if desired.
- Serve with the caramelized pineapple chunks and a side of rice or vegetables.

Enjoy your Pineapple and Ginger Pork Belly!

Tropical Mango Chutney Pork Tenderloin

Ingredients:

For the Pork Tenderloin:

- 1.5 lbs pork tenderloin
- 2 tbsp olive oil
- 1 tsp ground cumin
- 1 tsp paprika
- 1/2 tsp ground coriander
- 1/2 tsp garlic powder
- 1/2 tsp onion powder
- Salt and pepper to taste

For the Mango Chutney:

- 1 cup ripe mango, peeled and diced
- 1/4 cup red onion, finely chopped
- 1/4 cup bell pepper, finely chopped (red or yellow)
- 1/4 cup white sugar
- 2 tbsp apple cider vinegar
- 1 tbsp fresh ginger, grated
- 1 garlic clove, minced
- 1/4 tsp ground cinnamon
- 1/4 tsp ground turmeric
- 1/4 tsp chili flakes (optional, for heat)
- Salt to taste

Instructions:

1. **Prepare the Pork Tenderloin:**
    - Preheat your oven to 400°F (200°C).
    - In a small bowl, mix ground cumin, paprika, coriander, garlic powder, onion powder, salt, and pepper.
    - Rub the spice mixture all over the pork tenderloin.
    - Heat olive oil in a large ovenproof skillet over medium-high heat.
    - Sear the pork tenderloin on all sides until browned, about 2-3 minutes per side.
2. **Roast the Pork:**
    - Transfer the skillet with the pork tenderloin to the preheated oven.
    - Roast for 20-25 minutes, or until the internal temperature reaches 145°F (63°C).
    - Remove from the oven and let rest for 5 minutes before slicing.
3. **Make the Mango Chutney:**

- In a medium saucepan, combine diced mango, red onion, bell pepper, sugar, apple cider vinegar, ginger, garlic, cinnamon, turmeric, and chili flakes if using.
- Bring to a boil over medium heat, then reduce to a simmer.
- Cook for 15-20 minutes, stirring occasionally, until the mixture thickens and the mango is tender.
- Season with salt to taste.

4. **Serve:**
    - Slice the roasted pork tenderloin and serve with a generous spoonful of tropical mango chutney on top.
    - Garnish with fresh cilantro if desired.

Enjoy your Tropical Mango Chutney Pork Tenderloin!

www.ingramcontent.com/pod-product-compliance
Lightning Source LLC
LaVergne TN
LVHW081619060526
838201LV00054B/2318